EAT LIKE A LOCAL-BIRMINGHAM

*Birmingham United Kingdom
Food Guide*

Victoria Heath

CZYK Publishing Since 2011.

Eat Like a Local

Lock Haven, PA
All rights reserved.
ISBN: 9798662618749

BOOK DESCRIPTION

Are you excited about planning your next trip?

Do you want an edible experience? Would you like some culinary guidance from a local? If you answered yes to any of these questions, then this Eat Like a Local book is for you. Eat Like a Local - Birmingham, United Kingdom by Author Victoria Heath offers the inside scoop on food in Birmingham. Culinary tourism is an important aspect of any travel experience. Food has the ability to tell you a story of a destination, its landscapes, and culture on a single plate. Most food guides tell you how to eat like a tourist. Although there is nothing wrong with that, as part of the Eat Like a Local series, this book will give you a food guide from someone who has lived at your next culinary destination.

In these pages, you will discover advice on having a unique edible experience. This book will not tell you exact addresses or hours but instead will give you excitement and knowledge of food and drinks from a local that you may not find in other travel food guides.

Eat like a local. Slow down, stay in one place, and get to know the food, people, and culture. By the time you finish this book, you will be eager and prepared to travel to your next culinary destination.

OUR STORY

Traveling has always been a passion of the creator of the Eat Like a Local book series. During Lisa's travels in Malta, instead of tasting what the city offered, she ate at a large fast-food chain. However, she realized that her traveling experience would have been more fulfilling if she had experienced the best of local cuisines. Most would agree that food is one of the most important aspects of a culture. Through her travels, Lisa learned how much locals had to share with tourists, especially about food. Lisa created the Eat Like a Local book series to help connect people with locals which she discovered is a topic that locals are very passionate about sharing. So please join me and: Eat, drink, and explore like a local.

TABLE OF CONTENTS

DEDICATION

This book is dedicated to my Mum and Dad. Thank you for being my number one supporters, for teaching me that there is no ceiling to cap my dreams and for being the reason behind my drive and determination. This one's for you.

ABOUT THE AUTHOR

Victoria Heath is a student who likes nothing more than to write. Whether it be a single sentence that spurs her awake in the middle of the night, or an entire short story based off a brief encounter at a bus stop, Victoria finds the spark of writing at the heart of everything she does. She loves to travel too, with her dream to visit as many places as she can around the world; so it seemed a no-brainer to write about her home of Birmingham to show others what makes it so unique. Victoria has lived her entire life in the city, and as such has grown accustomed to some of the tips and tricks of getting around. She wants to share her knowledge with you, the reader, and hopefully pass on the message that, yes, - in the whirlwind of travel, Birmingham needs to be placed firmly on people's bucket lists of places to visit.

HOW TO USE THIS BOOK

The goal of this book is to help culinary travelers either dream or experience different edible experiences by providing opinions from a local. The author has made suggestions based on their own knowledge. Please do your own research before traveling to the area in case the suggested locations are unavailable.

Travel Advisories: As a first step in planning any trip abroad, check the Travel Advisories for your intended destination.
https://travel.state.gov/content/travel/en/traveladvisories/traveladvisories.html

FROM THE PUBLISHER

Traveling can be one of the most important parts of a person's life. The anticipation and memories that you have are some of the best. As a publisher of the *Eat Like a Local*, Greater Than a Tourist, as well as the popular *50 Things to Know* book series, we strive to help you learn about new places, spark your imagination, and inspire you. Wherever you are and whatever you do I wish you safe, fun, and inspiring travel.

Lisa Rusczyk Ed. D.
CZYK Publishing

*"One cannot think well, love
well, sleep well, if one has not
dined well."*

- Virginia Woolf

W hat makes a city a city? Yes, you have the towering buildings and hum of public transport, alongside the scurry of human life and endless interactions - but after all this, what really defines a place? Well, it's difficult to pinpoint exactly, but any city's unique qualities are almost certainly reflected in it's eateries. Food tells a story of the people, the culture - and it does so with just a few mouthfuls. What other resource can provide you with so much information about a place and be so moreish at the same time? But I know I don't need to win you over with these persuasive statements - after all, you're reading a food guide, so we're definitely on the same page (no pun intended).

If you needed any more convincing that food really is the heart of a place, read Virginia Woolf's quote at the start of this introduction. What a brilliant phrase. In such few words, Woolf describes the mechanics behind eating; the reason why good food turns our metaphorical cogs, and powers our very being.

The food we eat is more than simple nourishment; it tells a story, it paints a picture of a culture more richly than any canvas and ink could do. Eating like a local doesn't mean only dining at particularly well-known restaurants, nor does it mean forgoing anything that is less than culinary perfection. For me, eating like a local is exactly the opposite. It means exploring food as vastly as you can, in as many eateries as you can possibly fathom; eating not exclusively but inclusively, and obtaining as much experience as you can from the meal in front of you. It means searching high and low in the hopes you find that one brilliant place hidden in the nooks of the city.

And wouldn't you believe it, almost by magic, you're reading a book that does exactly that. A guide which narrows down the over eight hundred eateries in Birmingham into the best places to eat, with a few personal recommendations sprinkled in. This guide isn't by any means a compulsory, exclusive list of places to eat at. It's more a way of me nudging you and saying - 'Hey, this place is pretty great!' or

'Here's something you might not have heard about before.'.

Feel free to explore Birmingham as you please. After all, half the fun of being a tourist is the freedom of travelling (the other half comprises waking up without the blare of a 6'o'clock alarm, enjoying the good weather and cramming your suitcase full with souvenirs). Maybe the good weather in the UK is subjective, but that's a debate for another day.

I'll leave you to read the rest of this guide, and without further ado, get stuck in.

Birmingham
UK

Birmingham Climate

	High	Low
January	45	35
February	45	35
March	50	37
April	55	40
May	61	45
June	66	50
July	70	54
August	69	53
September	64	50
October	57	45
November	50	39
December	46	36

GreaterThanaTourist.com

Temperatures are in Fahrenheit degrees.
Source: NOAA

LET'S GO BACK TO THE BASICS

1. DON'T FORGET THE CASH (BUT CARDS ARE FINE TOO)

I decided to start this guide with several, more broad tips about Birmingham. Of course recommendations of eateries are expected in a food guide, but there's some equally important information that can't be condensed down into a list of restaurant names. My first tip is to always carry cash, as well as your cards, in Birmingham. Most places will happily accept card, contactless or cash payment, but there are several instances where you might only be able to pay cash, such as in smaller independent shops or in the Birmingham Indoor Market (paragraph here)

2. THERE'S LOADS OF SHOPPING CENTRES – VISIT THEM ALL

The city of Birmingham has several shopping centres; the Bullring, Grand Central and Piccadilly Arcade to name a few. There's so much to explore, it can be tempting to forgo some. Although you might expect them to be quite similar, each shopping centre is in fact vastly different. Expect to see different eateries and retail shops in each, and with every shopping centre comes a new atmosphere too. Visit as many as you can, and as the old saying goes - shop until you drop! (paragraph here)

3. USE PUBLIC TRANSPORT

It goes without saying that public transport is one of the greatest ways to navigate through a city. It can be fun to walk through a city, but don't forget about the extensive transport that Birmingham has to offer to help you along the way. Snow Hill train station by Colmore Row; the trams that run straight through Corporation Street; the constant influx of buses on Colmore Row and throughout the city - you'd be hard pressed to find a street in the city centre without any public transport at all. If you're planning on using any, download the Network West Midlands and National Express West Midlands apps. They are great tools for seeing live timetables, as well as having functions to see nearby stops. I've used the National Express West Midlands app countless times for buses. It saves the annoyance of waiting ages for a bus by telling you exactly when it will arrive, so you can relax knowing you won't have to run for it when it begins to drive off! (paragraph here)

4. EXPLORE THE CITY FIRST, THEN FIND THE FOOD

Although slightly contradictory to the conventions of a food guide, I think this is one of the most important factors to bear in mind when visiting any city - explore the place first, then let the food follow. I would recommend picking some of your favourite eateries to visit specifically, whilst other times freely exploring the city and seeing which restaurants, bars and cafés are near to you at that time. If you're near one of the places I've written about - that's great! - but don't panic if you're not near any eatery mentioned. Have a look on Trip Advisor and other food review websites, and if you're happy with the ratings, go for it. Don't limit yourself to the city centre of Birmingham either, simply because many of the restaurants listed in this guide are found there. Travelling is freedom, and I definitely recommend exploring past the locations listed in the guide if you stumble across a new, unfamiliar place (paragraph here)

CLASSIC BRITISH FOOD TO GET YOU STARTED

5. ENGLISH BREAKFASTS ARE A MUST

If you're visiting anywhere in the UK, you have to try an English breakfast, or a 'fry-up' as it's more commonly referred to. Expect to indulge in a hearty meal of sausages, bacon and fried egg, accompanied by sides of baked beans, tomatoes and mushrooms, and enjoy your fry-up with a hot drink of tea or coffee. Pop into The Hylton Cafe if you're near the Jewellery Quarter for a great breakfast, or Grand Central Kitchen, named aptly after its location in Grand Central. Their breakfasts are certainly hearty, but don't overlook Grand Central Kitchen's extensive lunch menu of paninis, baguettes and filled jacket potatoes too. Juju's Cafe, another great place for breakfast, offers vegetarian and vegan breakfasts, such as smashed avocado toasted muffins, veggie sausages with fried eggs, and vegan hash, alongside their traditional English breakfast menu. Bonus - Juju's Cafe also serves soft, warm pancakes with toppings such as bacon, syrup or berries. Mouth-watering! (paragraph here)

6. GET STUCK IN TO A ROAST DINNER

Sunday's were meant for roast dinners; the succulent, tender meat with potatoes and veg, served with lashings of gravy and sometimes, a hefty Yorkshire pudding to boot. The roast is high in the culinary ranks of British cuisine, alongside fish and chips and a good cup of tea - so if you want an authentic British experience, a roast needs to be on your list of things to eat. Anderson's Bar and Grill, in St Pauls Square, offers a Sunday roast menu on the last Sunday of each month. Three courses from the Sunday menu costs £25 for the meat option, or £20 for the vegetarian choice. Choose from a range of starters, from truffle beignets to classic prawn cocktail; mains such as roast turkey, wild mushroom with truffle cream sauce or Anderson's steak of the day; and indulge in sticky toffee pudding, fruit crumble or warm brownies for dessert. You can also find restaurants that serve roasts throughout the week, so feel free to indulge any day of the week.

The Old Crown is another great place for a tasty roast. Located in Digbeth, The Old Crown is the oldest secular building in Birmingham, with its existence being traced back to 1368. Their Sunday menu has a range of meats, from roast turkey to beef to succulent pork, which are all accompanied by roasted root vegetables and gravy. There are also vegan and vegetarian options, such as halloumi burgers or chestnut, squash and apricot roast. If you're still peckish, The Old Crown's dessert menu has traditional apple crumble and custard, as well as chocolate tortes and poached pears (paragraph here)

7. PUB GRUB – WHAT'S THE BIG DEAL?

Food served in a pub, or it's catchier term 'pub grub' has developed over the years, with most pubs serving hearty meals and extensive menus to enjoy alongside your beer and drinks. The dishes served are typically traditional English cuisine - think fish and chips, pies and sirloin steaks. For a proper pub experience, head down to The Old Joint Stock, where you'll also find an 100-seat theatre with a huge programme of events. The venue is uniquely decorated in lavish Victorian decor, with a glass-domed roof and island bar. The Old Joint Stock is the perfect combination of good pub grub and an intimate, atmospheric location (paragraph here)

8. AFTERNOON TEA FIT FOR ROYALTY

Another great British experience is the afternoon tea. Expect to be served scones with lashings of cream and jam, miniature sandwiches and other finger food. All this delicious food is usually accompanied by a pot of tea or alcoholic drinks depending on what package you opt for. For a traditional afternoon tea, try 1565 Restaurant Bar & Terrace, where you can enjoy your tea outside on their terrace. Their menu offers treats such as raspberry and white chocolate lollipops, Boston turkey relish cobs and Pimm's sorbet. And to top it off, there's a great choice of specially-sourced teas to pick from to accompany your afternoon tea.

Just outside of the city centre of Birmingham lies The Edgbaston Boutique Hotel and Cocktail Lounge, which offers a stunning afternoon tea in elegant surroundings. Choose from a selection of scrumptious sandwiches and sweet treats, including the classic scone served with strawberry jam and Cornish clotted cream. The teas on offer are certainly unique - pick from flavours such as Lemon Verbena, Jasmine Silver Needle or Vanilla Black. If you prefer cold drinks, The Edgbaston Hotel also offers a selection of ice teas, such as Rosy Cheeks (Turkish Rose), Spring Greens (matcha green tea with lemon, pear and apple) and Vanilla Assam Tea with pressed apple and lemon. You can also opt to have your afternoon tea with a glass of Champagne, wine or gin-infused cocktails served in vintage crockery.

But if you're looking for a twist on the classic afternoon tea, Zindiya is the place to be. Their menu offers a 'High Chai', which combines Indian spices in both teas and food, with dishes such as homemade cardamom scones, seasonal macarons and bombay sandwiches to choose from. Their teas range from masala chai to very berry to English breakfast, so there's a flavour for everyone (paragraph here)

9. LIKE A KID IN A SWEET SHOP

A classic British high-street favourite - the sweet shop. The tubs of coloured sweets, stacked as high as the ceiling, you really do feel like a child once you step into one of these. As the years have passed, most traditional sweet shops have faded away, but there still remains a few in our high-streets. One to certainly visit is Mr Simms Olde Sweet Shoppe, which offers a variety of sweets in Victorian-style stores. Located in the Great Western Arcade, the old-worldly style sweet shop fits in perfectly with the quaint exteriors of many of the shops in the shopping destination. Choose from classics such as lemon sherbets, pear drops or rhubarb and custards, as well as more modern varieties like mega sour fruits (paragraph here)

10. YOU HAVE TO VISIT A CHIPPY

Another firm favourite in the UK is fish and chips. There are a number of English restaurants which offer the staple meal, but I think for the most authentic taste, you should head to an actual fish and chip shop or fondly named 'chippy'. No other place can replicate freshly battered cod and chips like a fish and chip shop can. Some of the best chippies in Birmingham include Dad's Lane Fish Bar and Pisces Fish Bar, but there are so many of them around the city.

Chippies do not typically have sit-down, in store dining, so that's something to bear in mind if you're looking for a proper sit-down meal. Customers often eat their food straight from the paper or trays they are served in or order food to enjoy at home. There are other things to eat other than the classic fish and chips, such as sausage in batter, kebabs and fishcakes, which are all served at most chip shops. For any vegetarians, try the Veggie Chippy, which serves vchicken (veggie soy chicken), battered veggie soy fish fingers and pastas to name a few dishes. They also offer vchicken bucket deals, which can be customised to be regular or tandoori flavoured.

Whilst you're in the Midlands, you have to try orange chips for a taste of pure, salt-and-vinegary heaven. No, the chips have no wacky relations to the citrus fruit - orange chips refer to the crispy, orange batter which the traditional chips are covered in. They're crunchy, flavoursome and enjoyed best eaten straight out of the packet with a little plastic fork (paragraph here)

11. DON'T FORGET ABOUT THE PIE

The pie is arguably one of the cornerstones of British culinary delights, so choosing the best one to dine on is a big decision. Although you will find a pie on most menus in British restaurants, there's one place in particular that does the golden crust and filling combo perfectly, and that is Pieminister. The restaurant offers individual pies served with gravy, as well as pie meals (your choice of pie accompanied by mushy pies, chips and a whole load of other tempting sides). There's the classic British beef and ale pie, as well as flavours like chicken, bacon and tarragon to choose from. You can customise your pie to be gluten-free, and there are also vegan pies available such as mushroom, tomato and quinoa. If you have room for more, Pieminister offers a selection of soft-serve sundaes for dessert, as well as hot puddings like chocolate cake and sticky toffee pudding (paragraph here)

12. A 99 ICE CREAM

If you're visiting Birmingham during late spring or summer, you can expect to see ice-cream vans around local parks in the area, such as Cannon Hill Park. One of the best things you can ask for from the van is a 99 ice cream or 'whippy'. Essentially, it is soft-serve vanilla ice cream in a wafer cone served with a Flake (a type of Cadbury's chocolate) placed into the top. It sounds simple - and it is - but there's something so satisfying about that creamy, chocolate combination that has kept it a firm favourite in Britain for many years. And it's the perfect treat to eat in the warm weather - what's not to love? (paragraph here)

BIRMINGHAM SPECIALTIES

13. THE HOME OF THE BIRMINGHAM BALTI

You might be surprised to find out that the origins of the balti stem from Birmingham, where you can find the much-loved, familiar curry in many balti houses around the city. Perhaps the most renowned of all balti houses is Adil's, whose owner Mohammed Arif came up with the idea of the balti itself. The balti house describes itself as 'pioneers of the balti cuisine', and certainly lives up to any expectations. The menu is filled with delights like succulent sharing platters of samosas and tandoori seafood, tropical baltis and fragrant biryanis. There is a kids menu, too, with dishes such as omelettes and chicken nuggets, as well as half-portions of their famous balti.

Now, although this next eatery is slightly outside of Birmingham, I would feel as though I'm keeping a gem of a place to myself if I didn't share it. My family and I have been ordering from Balti Herbs and Spices for over 25 years, and each order of fragrant curries, naan bread and sundries just confirms that this is the best Indian takeaway by a mile. Although there is no sit-down table service, they offer both collection and delivery. If you are to indulge in one takeaway in your trip to Birmingham, Balti Herbs and Spices is the place to go. Trust me on this one. Seriously. (P.S: my favourite dish from there is chicken pathia with keema naan and pilau rice - you have to try it) (paragraph here)

14. IF YOU HAVEN'T TRIED PORK SCRATCHINGS, YOU SHOULD

Seriously, you have to get your hands on some of these. Quite simply, pork scratchings are fried pig skins, seasoned with salt and other flavourings. You'll be able to find pork scratchings in pre-packaged bags at smaller convenience shops, as well as larger chains such as Asda or Tesco. There's different types of pork scratchings as well; harder and more crispy, or puffy with a texture like popcorn. Try a few different varieties to see which one you like the best - they are generally not more than £1 a bag - so eat your heart out! (paragraph here)

15. THAT BUILDING WITH THE SILVER DOTS

If you have walked into the city centre, you might be wondering what the futuristic building covered in silver dots is. That is Selfridges, where amongst its floors of luxury clothing and homeware lies an extensive and sometimes overlooked food hall. And if you go there at the right times, (hint: near to closing time on weeknight evenings), you might even pick up a bargain from some of the food outlets. I've managed to buy decadent, gooey brownies for only 99p from bakeries, when they've been sold only hours before at £3.50 a slice. And if you're impartial to a sweet treat, Blondie's Kitchen (also in Selfridges) sells warm, chewy cookies as well as other baked goods, all served with a glass of milk. 'Try before you buy' is a great motto, and Blondie's Kitchen certainly lives up to it - they regularly offer samples of baked delights on their counters to try. Selfridges Food Hall also offers goodies such as pre-packaged condiment sets, personalised Nutella jars and traditional tin boxes of English tea, so if you want to take home a foodie souvenir or two, you've got it all covered here.

If you're looking to sit down after a long day of shopping, however, Selfridges boasts several restaurants and cafés too. Some are larger, such as Ed's Easy Diner (an American diner) or Yo! (which serves Japanese street-food and sushi. Whereas others, such as Tonkotsu (a ramen bar) are smaller chains - fun fact: it is the first Tonkotsu outside of London. (paragraph here)

16. STREET FOOD FOR EVERY TASTE

If you want to immerse yourself in the eateries of Birmingham, there's no better place to start than Digbeth Dining Club. Meander around the huge selection of stalls and venues, which change regularly, to find food and drink from a whole host of tempting cuisines. The plethora of street food, ranging from succulent meat to mouth-watering Caribbean delights, means you're only a stall away from discovering your new favourite meal. Plus - all this delicious food is accompanied by music and a vibrant, energetic atmosphere. Digbeth Dining Club is a brilliant way to start pushing your culinary boundaries in Birmingham, as you can try many different cuisines all in one place (paragraph here)

17. A CHRISTMAS MARKET LIKE NO OTHER

If you choose to visit Birmingham in late November or December, you can visit the largest German market in Europe outside of Austria or Germany. Take your pick from numerous flavours of chocolate covered marshmallows; flavoursome doughnuts or iced gingerbread. A personal sweet favourite of mine is the Kinder Bueno crêpe; warm, gooey chocolate surrounded by a soft, freshly prepared crêpe. There's so many more flavours to choose from, but after several years of visiting the German Market, Kinder Bueno remains number one for me. And for the savoury fanatics, a Frankfurt hot-dog with potato fries is a must, or a foot-long feat if you can manage to eat it all. If you're feeling thirsty, pop over to one of the many stalls that sprawl across the city centre to enjoy a glass of mulled wine, beer or warm hot chocolate. Enjoy your food whilst exploring the craft stalls that the market has, offering gifts such as hand-crafted baubles, homeware and children's toys. There's some festive sing-a-longs throughout the night, so be sure to find the action and enjoy yourself (paragraph here)

18. LAST BUT NOT LEAST, THE BIRMINGHAM MARKETS

The Birmingham markets are the best place to go if you want a bargain. The outdoor markets feature a typical grocer's selections of fruits, vegetables and pre-packaged goods at an affordable price. There's also stalls which sell fabrics and clothing, so have a look around the entire market to see what takes your fancy. The indoor markets are mostly fish and meat counters, selling fresh produce at reasonable prices compared to their high-street competitors. Feel free to haggle with the stall owners - it is common practice to ask for a lowered price in the markets, and more often than not, you can haggle the price down by a few pounds (paragraph here)

BARS AND PUBS WITH GREAT FOOD TO MATCH

19. IS IT A DRINK OR A SCIENCE EXPERIMENT?

Cocktails in a conical flask; a huge tower of foam atop of a strawberry daiquiri; steam billowing from your glass - it all sounds quite like a scene from Alice In Wonderland, but you'd be very wrong to think this is all fantasy. This crazy combination of theatrical presentation and cocktails is the work of The Alchemist in Birmingham, whose menu is packed with brilliant drinks and food. There's cocktails for every taste; whether you choose a classic mojito or frozen strawberry daiquiri, or want a dry-ice extravaganza in the form of Mad Hatters. The Alchemist serves cocktails that quite literally change colour in front of your eyes, as well as smoking, blood-red drinks (aptly named Dead Red Zombie). If you're not a cocktail fan, The Alchemist also offers wine, prosecco and non-alcoholic drinks to satisfy any taste. The fun doesn't stop at the drinks though - there's a full appetising menu and bar nibbles to pick from, such as vegetarian and meat sharing platters, homemade falafel wraps and tasty fish-finger sandwiches (a truly British dish!). The wonderfully unique flavours don't stop at the cocktails, with desserts such as chocolate brownies, sweet gyozas and cotton candy baked Alaska appearing on the menu. You can also book cocktail masterclasses for 6-12 people, and really get stuck into the creation of some marvellous drinks. The Alchemist is a must-go for any cocktail lover, who wants not only a great drink but an experience to match (paragraph here)

20. STRAIGHT OUT OF A STORYBOOK

The classic tale of Dr Jekyll and Mr Hyde is brought to life in one of Birmingham's most unusual gin and cocktail bars, located in the Colmore Business District - Jekyll And Hyde. Enjoy a collection of cocktails served alongside around one hundred global gins, or instead, head upstairs to the Parlour to enjoy a seasonal cocktail menu surrounded by extravagant Victorian decor. The theme of the book continues into the bar menu, with dishes such as Dr Jekyll's Pie (beef, ale and mushroom) and Mr Hyde's Pie (roasted root vegetables in Béchamel sauce) on offer. The bar also serves an extensive range of craft ales, boutique bottled beer and soft drinks as an alternative to cocktails (paragraph here)

21. BOTTOMLESS BRUNCH – YES, THAT INCLUDES ALCOHOL

That's right - bottomless alcohol. Sounds like a dream? Well, I bet you're pleased to know this is a very real reality at Aluna in Birmingham, and you can enjoy some great food alongside equally brilliant cocktails and prosecco. Choose from mains such as eggs florentine, traditional breakfast and Aluna buttermilk waffle, and finish off with a dessert of brownies, pancakes or waffles. The bottomless drinks available are classic prosecco and pornstar martinis, and the more unusual bubblegum-tini. Aluna also offers a more extensive normal cocktail and food menu if you don't fancy a brunch (paragraph here)

22. BEERS TO MATCH YOUR MEAL

Wind down at the Purecraft Bar and Kitchen, where you'll find a menu with over 75 types of bottled beer, real ales on tap and hearty food. Their food menu includes dishes such as rarebits, onion rings and rump cap steak, with some items on the menu being paired with a specific recommendation of beer to accompany your meal. The recommendation is entirely optional, but if you're feeling overwhelmed by the choice of drinks, Purecraft has you covered with their personal pairing. If you're not too peckish, tuck into some of their traditional British snacks such as pork pies, home roasted nuts and sausage rolls, which are all available to purchase at their bar.

INDULGE IN TASTES FAR AND WIDE

23. COME ALONG TO THE CHINESE QUARTER

Birmingham's culture extends far and wide, and the Chinese Quarter is definitely one of the places to go to experience this. Expect to see streets lined with Chinese, Korean and Japanese eateries selling delicious authentic food. There's so many places in the Chinese Quarter to choose from, so I've tried to narrow it down into some of the best eateries to go to.

One of my favourite places to eat is Ming Moon, a Pan-Asian buffet-style restaurant. There's such a large selection of food to choose from, that it would be impossible to list it all here. Some of my favourites that I've tried are duck pancakes and beef stir fry with noodles. I feel it's important to mention they have a chocolate fountain and a whippy ice-cream machine (maybe I'm easily impressed but it blew me away when I saw it), and as it's a buffet, you can eat until your heart's content. But like I said before, there is honestly so much food to choose from, so you really have to go to Ming Moon to fully experience it yourself.

Tattu is another great place to eat in the Chinese Quarter, where you can dine on Chinese cuisine such as sweet and sour vegetable tempura, chilli salt baby squid and crispy shredded chilli beef. You can pick from a range of small or large plates, or eat from a set menu delivered in 'waves' to the table. The best part about Tattu has to be the decor of the place - cherry blossom hangs in huge plumes from the ceiling, and the whole restaurant is dimly lit, creating such a relaxed atmosphere.

The Chinese Quarter doesn't just stop at restaurants though; there are many bakeries in the area too. Head down to Wah Kee Bakery, where you can choose from over twenty types of baked goods such as egg tarts and cheesecakes. Browse through their daily cake collections of Dark Forest and Matcha cakes, or buy personalised birthday cakes for special occasions. Wah Kee Bakery also sells bubble tea, which is brewed with fresh milk, leaves and fruit, in flavours such as sweet pineapple, smashed tarro and cheese rose (paragraph here)

24. BIRMINGHAM'S BEST VEGAN EATERIES

Birmingham has several vegan restaurants and eateries, one of which is aptly named Vegan Munch. The eatery specialises in wraps and juices, with their menu including flavoursome dishes such as spiced vegan doner kebab, vegan shawarma and 'not' chicken fillet burgers. The juices on offer are equally as delicious, with flavour like Pineapple Sunset, Strawberry Delight and Zucchini Energia. Another great vegan eatery is Natural Bar and Kitchen, which is Birmingham's first vegan bar and kitchen. Their

menu is split into a la carte and buffet, with tofu fish
and chips, ramen bowls and barbecue jackfruit
sandwiches just some of the selection to choose from.
There's even an option for self service - fill your plate
with as much food as you want, then weigh it and pay
at the bar. Plant-based desserts at Natural Bar And
Kitchen truly pack a punch with their flavour too;
expect tasty delights such as key lime pie, pistachio
and rose torte and lemon chia pudding (paragraph
here)

25. A SLICE OF HEAVEN

The pizza - need I say more? The classic dish with
its soft base, cheesy crust and moreish toppings
remains a firm favourite food of many. One of the
best places to go for pizza in Birmingham is @pizza,
located in Grand Central. Choose from their range of
freshly-prepared, hand-crafted pizzas or customise
your own pizza from a range of fifty ingredients. Pre-
designed pizzas include classics such as margarita,
hot'n'spicy and meaty. There's two pizzas in
particular, however, that are far different to your
average cheese and tomato. First is the 'Trunchbull',
a doughy, pizza-dessert hybrid that is perfect for any

chocolate lovers. Expect a sweet pizza base topped with sweet ricotta, chocolate and mascarpone served with a drizzle of raspberry coulis and icing sugar. If you want to combine breakfast and pizza all in one, however, order the 'At Tiffany's' pizza, which adds toppings like egg, Italian sausage and bacon to a cheese and tomato base (paragraph here)

26. DINE ACROSS THE ATLANTIC

Take a trip to the States whilst visiting Birmingham by visiting Coast To Coast on Broad Street, where you can expect to indulge in hearty American classics. Begin your culinary trip across the Atlantic with appetisers such as loaded nachos, spicy calamari and chicken wings. Then, enjoy mains of pulled pork and slaw burgers, racks of succulent buffalo ribs and mac'n'cheese, as well as milkshakes in flavours such as vanilla and mint choc chip to accompany your food. The full works of American dining continues into the desserts, where buttermilk pancakes, cookie cheesecake and salted caramel pecan pie feature on the menu (paragraph here)

27. WATCH THE WORLD GO BY WITH A COFFEE

There's something uniquely comforting about sitting in a coffee shop, drink in hand, watching the world go by. Birmingham is full of chain coffee shops, for example Starbucks and Costa serving classic iced and hot brews. However, if you're looking for a more intimate and relaxed experience, head to Faculty Coffee And Tea in Piccadilly Arcade. The coffee shop is laid-back, relaxed and above all else a great supplier of the beloved hot drink. Choose from guest roasts with interesting names like Square Mile Coffee Roasters or Quarter Horse Coffee, and pick from a range of cakes and pastries supplied by the bakery next-door, Sixteen (paragraph here)

28. TAKE A PIT STOP IN HAWAII

Come along to Kuula Poké for a trip straight to Hawaii, where you'll be met with a fusion of exotic flavours and fresh ingredients. This restaurant serves vibrant poké bowls, which are a healthy combination of sushi fish, meats or tofu and rice. Expect layers of vegetables and tropical fruits within your bowl, all topped with a mixture of sauces and sprinkles. You can order from their pre-set menu, or customise your very own poké bowl. First, choose from a base of coconut brown rice, white sushi rice or courgette noodles. Then, begin to add layers with a choice of fish, huli huli tofu or poached chicken, and add toppings such as mango, seaweed and hickory carrot. The bowl is finally completed with a choice of sauce or mayo, as well as sprinklings of chilli flakes, crispy shallots and coconut 'bacon'. The restaurant also serves açai and smoothie bowls, with refreshing flavours such as dragon fruit and strawberry pear, matcha smoothie and classic açai (paragraph here)

29. GREAT THAI FOOD THAT PACKS A PUNCH

Siamias, located in Brindleyplace, is the perfect place to go if you're looking for a meal full of flavour and spices. Choose from mains such as chargrilled king tiger prawns served with Thai chilli sauce, stir-fried beef in oyster sauce and mixed vegetables in satay. There's a whole host of sides to pick from too, with prawn crackers, stir-fried noodles and steamed jasmine rice all featuring on the menu.The desserts at Siamias are also full of refreshing flavours, with dishes such as mango and red berry mousse, coconut sorbet and lemon and ginger cheesecake. I find their menu to be quite helpful, with little skulls printed next to each dish as a note of how spicy the dish is (the more skulls there are, the more spicy the meal is!) (paragraph here)

30. STEAK, STEAK AND MORE STEAK

For all the meat-lovers, you will be pleased to know Birmingham is home to some amazing steakhouses that serve succulent, prime steaks accompanied with flavoursome side dishes. Try out some of the best steaks at Fiesta Del Asado, an Argentinian restaurant located in both Solihull and Edgbaston. Their range of premium steaks includes soft and lean beef sirloin, a forty ounce beef costilla for two and grilled pork flank steak. Each steak is brushed with Fiesta Del Asado's house baste and served with fries, which you can upgrade to chunky chips if you would prefer.

If you're in the city centre, try out Gaucho, another Argentinian steakhouse serving some of the finest Argentinian steaks. The decor inside in the restaurant pays homage to Argentina's forests, with sophisticated textures and colours to really immerse you into the experience. Their steaks come from Black Angus cattle (a premium type), which are bred in Argentina at farms that the restaurant has partnered with for many years. Begin by choosing from a range of steaks such as sirloin, fillet and ribeye, then choose your size (ranging from 225g-400g). Finish off your steak with a choice of sauces and jus, as well as toppings such as truffle and black pepper butter (paragraph here)

31. EAT YOUR HEART OUT AT THIS ITALIAN EATERY

Fogo Bar and Kitchen is an Italian restaurant which serves homemade wood oven pizza, pasta and other traditional Italian dishes. All of their recipes are inspired by the traditions of Italian cooking, so you can be sure to enjoy authentic, fresh tastes in any dish you choose. Classics such as spaghetti bolognese, seafood risotto and margarita pizza are included on the menu, as well as starters such as Italian olives, garlic bread and salt and pepper squid. Accompany your meal with Fogo Bar and Kitchen's large variety of Italian wines and beers, specifically selected to complement your meal (paragraph here)

32. INDULGE IN SOME AUTHENTIC JAPANESE FOOD

I'm getting straight to the point with this tip - you need to eat at Yakinori whilst on your trip to Birmingham. There's a few Yakinori's dotted around Birmingham, with the one in the city centre being located in Grand Central. The restaurant serves fresh sushi, grilled teriyaki and katsu curry amongst other traditional Japanese food. The dish you need to try, however, is chicken and prawn chilli noodles. The combination of spiced stir-fried noodles with crispy vegetables and succulent meat is so moreish, and the noodles are freshly prepared to order too. What's not to love? (paragraph here)

33. THE BEST BURGERS IN BIRMINGHAM

The classic beef burger can be found in most restaurants in the UK, but there's something uniquely moreish about the burgers at Original Patty Men that keeps customers coming back for more. The menu includes the much-loved cheeseburger topped with lettuce, white onion and Boss Man sauce, as well as twists on the classic such as burgers with pineapple hot sauce and deep fried chicken thigh burgers served with lime and ginger slaw. They also offer a deep fried pickled tofu burger, which is suitable for vegans. Finish off your tasty burger with a side of naked or skin-on fries, which can be seasoned with a choice of spice mix (paragraph here)

34. TRY OUT SOME BAO

Bao is a type of yeast-leavened bun popular in Chinese cuisine, which is typically steamed and served with a range of different fillings. There's a great eatery that sells Bao in Grand Central, called Tiger Bites Pig. Expect bao filled with flavours such as beef chilli, chicken with spring onion and ginger, and tofu and aubergine, or choose a rice bowl with moreish chicken and salt and pepper tofu. Eateries in Grand Central are great for on-the-go snacks whilst shopping, or as a quick meal if you're about to catch that all-important train from the station! (paragraph here)

SOME HIDDEN GEMS

35. A CINEMA AND A RESTAURANT IN ONE PLACE

Both places that I'm about to talk about in this section are located in the Custard Factory in Digbeth, just a few minutes walk from the Bullring. I'll mention the Custard Factory in one of my bonus tips in the later part of the guide, but take my word now - it should definitely be on your list of places to visit. There's so much to explore in this unique, urban area of Birmingham, including some fantastic eateries. One of the more unusual is Mockingbird Cinema and Kitchen, which, as you may have guessed, combines great tasting gourmet food with a cinema all in the same place. Their menu includes dishes such as grilled and fried chicken breast with fries, vegan bean patties and plant-based meatballs. If this moreish menu wasn't enough, certain showings are accompanied by bespoke themed food to enhance your cinema experience (paragraph here)

36. GREAT FOOD, GREAT NUTRITION, GREAT TASTE

Kanteen is a healthy restaurant which prides itself on serving food that doesn't compromise either nutrition or flavour. Choose from their range of salad boxes, with dishes such as curried cauliflower couscous and thai rice noodles with slaw and satay sauce, as well as choices of hot boxes and toast with wonderful, exotic toppings. They offer breakfast, lunch and dinner, so pop in at any time of the day for a tasty meal (paragraph here)

FINE DINING

37. DID SOMEONE SAY 'MICHELIN STAR'?

Michelin star dining was never easier to find in a city. Birmingham has several Michelin Star restaurants, all of which have particularly different food offerings. One of the most well-known is Adam's Restaurant, a British fine-dining restaurant with excellent ratings from AA, Trip Advisor and The Good Food Guide. In 2019, Adam's was rated the number one restaurant in the UK, and tenth in the world by Trip Advisor. Adam's, alongside most fine-dining restaurants, comes with a typically higher price (a three-course meal will set you back £75), but arguably, the prices are reflected in the exquisite food you receive. Choose from lunch, tasting and three-course menus with great gourmet dishes such as scallops, suckling pig and banana soufflé.

However, if you're looking to try high-quality Indian cuisine, Opheem is definitely the place to go. Browse through their lunch a la carte menu, or try a bit of everything in their 5 or 8 course tasting menus (£65 and £85 respectively). Two courses from their lunch menu will cost £30, which is served with half a bottle of house wine or a non-alcoholic cocktail. You can expect dishes such as rich curries, accompanied by garlic naan and steamed rice, as well as mouth-watering tandoori duck breasts and fresh sorbets. Opheem also offers an extensive wine, liquor and port menu alongside their food, as well as as a cocktail bar with experienced bartenders to create your perfect drink.

Another brilliant Michelin Star restaurant is Restaurant Folium, near St Paul's Square, which is best described as a modern British restaurant. Restaurant Folium offers food with simple appearances that are rich in high-quality ingredients and flavour, with their menu changing regularly depending on the ingredients available. Devonshire smoked eel, Cornish duck with dried plums and lavender honey and sheep yogurt sorbet are only a handful of dishes from their Spring/Summer Menu. Prices range from £27.50 for a two-course lunch, to £80 for a seven-course dinner (paragraph here)

38. IF YOU LOVE SEAFOOD, LOOK NO FURTHER

The Oyster Club is the best place to go if you're a seafood fanatic. The restaurant is in fact owned by the same individuals as Adam's, the Michelin star restaurant that I mentioned above. As the name suggests, The Oyster Club serves a range of fresh oysters with dressings at its very own Oyster Bar. But don't let that fool you into thinking oysters are the only seafood served here - the restaurant offers dishes such as fish pie with lobster, skate wing and dressed white crab, as well as a delicious dessert menu (paragraph here)

A MEAL WITH A VIEW

39. DINE NEARBY THE CANALSIDE

Birmingham is a city of duality; boasting the grandeur of typical city-life, as well as the quaint atmosphere of canals and river-boats. One of the benefits of this is the ability to eat in both types of places - you can immerse yourself in the bustle or equally, the elegant quiet of the canalside. There are several restaurants which overlook Birmingham's canals, such as Gas Street Social in the Mailbox. Expect to dine on brunches and European sharing plates, served alongside a traditional family atmosphere. Gas Street Social also offers a weekday set-menu with excellent prices - two courses for £13.50 or three courses for £15.50. The dishes to choose from aren't limited by any means - salt and pepper squid, Caesar salad and gammon steaks to name a few. But if you're looking to try some traditional British food, Malt House is the place to be. The menu includes classics such as steak and ale pies, sausages and mash and fish and chips. The Malt House is also nearby the Utilita Arena, a popular concert venue, as well as the Sea Life Centre. If you're visiting either, the Malt House is in the perfect location for a bite to eat and drink (paragraph here)

40. OR EAT YOUR MEAL UP HIGH

If high-quality dining with a birds-eye view of Birmingham sounds like a treat, you must pay a visit to Marco Pierre White's Steakhouse, Bar & Grill. Enjoy the stunning views of the city whilst you dine on gourmet food, such as grilled swordfish and beef steaks, freshly-ground burgers grilled to order and chicken madras curry. Desserts range from rich chocolate mousse to a refreshing strawberries and cream vanilla panna cotta (paragraph here)

QUICK BITES TO EAT AND DRINK

41. WRAP IT UP

If you're in the middle of a shopping spree around the Bullring and don't fancy sitting down for a full meal, visit Wrap Chic on the top floor. The eatery is best described as a fusion between Indian and Mexican food, with their dishes combining the most exciting flavours of both. Choose from a range of tortillas, wraps and bowls, all served with rice and salad alongside your choice of filling (chicken tikka, soya amritsari and chicken methi to name a few). There's also a range of tasty sides available, such as wrapchips (oven-cooked potato wedges), wraposas (samosas with your choice of filling) and spicy chicken wings (paragraph here)

42. CAN I TEMPT YOU WITH SOME BUBBLE TEA?

Bubble tea has become increasingly popular in the past few years, with many places popping up all over the city centre specialising in the delicious drink. One of the most popular places to get bubble tea is Mee-

Cha in the Bullring, where you can enjoy a range of milky or fruity flavours for your tea. Mee-Cha also sells fruit slushies that can be customised with your choice of toppings, as well as a range of frozen yogurts and ice-creams. If you're around the Chinese Quarter, head to Happy Lemon for a taste of authentic bubble tea. Happy Lemon follows a series of steps for your perfect drink; firstly, choose your drink, size and temperature. Next, pick your choice of toppings; and finally, choose your sweetness and ice level. Talk about a custom drink! You're guaranteed to love it (paragraph here)

43. A BAKERY LIKE NO OTHER

If you love freshly baked bread and meringues, go to Bread Collection in the Great Western Arcade, which overlooks Colmore Row (note: they only accept cash!) Walk in to a rather quaint, rustic shop, with stacks of freshly baked bread and other goods. The bread is amazing, it is so soft and fluffy, with flavours such as sundried tomato, rye and sunflower and sourdough to choose from. The Bread Collection also sells some of the best meringues I've ever tasted. Now, when I say they are big, I'm not exaggerating.

These meringues are absolutely huge! They are the epitome of a perfect meringue - a crunchy exterior with a soft, melt-in-your-mouth centre. I've only tried the raspberry flavour, but there are lots more to pick from (paragraph here)

44. SWEET TOOTHED HEAVEN

For all you sweet-toothed foodies out there, I've got your back. My all-time favourite sweet treat in Birmingham is a warm cinnamon sugar pretzel from Mr Pretzel. They also offer other sweet and savoury flavours, such as chocolate, cheese and pizza - but the cinnamon sugar one remains the best in my opinion. Another great sweet treat to try is cronut from Dum Dum Doughnuts in Grand Central. The strange sounding item is in fact a hybrid of a croissant and doughnut - think the flakey layers of a croissant with the sweet, sticky texture of a doughnut. They're absolutely delicious and a must-try if you're in Grand Central, especially since Dum Dum Doughnuts is the world's first creator of the baked cronut.

Branching out from the city centre is Stickie Fingers, found in Digbeth, which serves tempting ranges of American pancakes served with your choice of toppings (both savoury and sweet), as well as doughnuts stacked high with chocolatey treats.

And finally, if you're looking for an ice-cream that packs a punch, head down to LA Pop in Edgbaston where you can make your own personalised ice-cream lolly. Start by choosing your flavour from chocolate to blood orange sorbet to just milk, and add your choice of toppings to complete the lolly. LA Pop also sells cheesecake pops and dipped strawberries, so there's certainly a sweet treat to suit everyone's taste (paragraph here)

45. BLEND IT ALL UP

There's nothing better than a cold, refreshing smoothie or juice to quench your thirst. And with Birmingham being such a large city, it's expected that there's a few places to choose from. One of my favourites is Fuel, located in both Grand Central and the Bullring. They sell a range of juices and smoothies, ranging from fruit crushes to super smoothies which can be blended with whey protein or other supplements. The best one I've tried is definitely Raspberry Crush; a blend of apple juice, raspberries and fat free sorbet.

However, if you're looking to enjoy your juice alongside a meal, Joe and The Juice is the perfect place for you. Their range of shakes and juices is extensive, with flavours such as Herb Tonic, Choco Shake and Fibre Active to choose from. And their food menu is just as flavoursome, with dishes like acai bowls, roasted chickpea and pomegranate salads and spicy tuna sandwiches (paragraph here)

EAT WITH AN EXPERIENCE

46. CRAZY GOLF, LESS CRAZY FOOD

A cross-over that trumps all else - introducing Ghetto Golf, a venue which combines 18-hole crazy golf, a cocktail bar and flavoursome food all under one roof. Ghetto Golf's interior is covered in bold, vibrant graffiti and artwork, reflecting the urban style of its location in Digbeth. Have a great night out whilst dining on moreish burgers, loaded fries and tapas - and don't forget to check out their range of

excellent cocktails and alcoholic drinks too
(paragraph here)

47. CADBURY'S WORLD IS A MUST

Cadbury's chocolate is arguably the most iconic confectionery to come from the United Kingdom. And who could believe it - its origins are right here in Birmingham - so it comes as no surprise that the beloved chocolate has its own visitor attraction. Take a trip to Cadbury's World for a day out that combines chocolate with a great learning experience - why can't all classrooms be like this? If you ever wanted to try Cadbury's chocolate, you will certainly get enough of it here. There is an admissions charge, but once you're inside, expect to be given free bars of chocolate along your self-guided tour. For an extra charge, treat yourself to a Cadbury's World Chocolatier Experience, where you'll learn the history behind chocolate making as well as trying out your own chocolate handwriting skills.

And don't forget about the gift shop on this day out. There's chocolate in pretty much every form -

bars, individually wrapped sweets and so much more. The gift shop is the world's largest Cadbury's store - and the best part? - you don't have to pay the main attraction entry fee to come inside. I would recommend taking home some classic Dairy Milk chocolate, as well as my all-time-favourite Roses (a selection of wrapped chocolates with tasty fillings) (paragraph here)

VALUE FOR MONEY

48. BUY A TESCO MEAL DEAL

I was tempted to title this as 'The Great British Bargain', as I am that passionate that Tesco's Meal Deal is one of the best bargains you can get on the High Street. Although not by any means the greatest food you can eat, the Tesco Meal Deal is perfect for an on-the-go, satisfying (and did I mention value for money?!) meal. For only £3, you can choose from a variety of pre-packaged main meals, snacks and drinks to make your own meal. It comprises of three sections - the main, the side and the drink. The range of items available in the Meal Deal is so extensive, ranging from vegetable sushi, ham sandwiches and pasta to fruit bowls, crisps and juices. And for only £3, regardless of which three items you pick, you can save a decent amount of money. There is a Tesco in the city centre, stocked full of choices to pick from for your Meal Deal (paragraph here)

49. GO TO GREGGS FOR A SAUSAGE ROLL

A sausage roll might not be on your list of delicacies to eat, but those warm, flakey pastries from Gregg's really fit the phrase 'cheap and cheerful'. Gregg's is a high-street chain of bakeries which sells baked goods, hot drinks and meal deals at an affordable cost. There's so much more to Gregg's than the sausage roll, but if there's one thing you buy from there, it needs to be this (there's also a vegan sausage roll which I've heard is quite tasty) (paragraph here)

50. THE ONLY WAY IS SUBWAY

This much-loved sandwich eatery has stores in Birmingham, and it's no secret how tasty their food is. There's always meal deals and offers available, so if you're lucky you can grab a sandwich, drink and side for under £5. Subway has expanded their menu to include salads, wraps and nachos too, all at a great price. Eating well doesn't always have to break the bank, and the food you get can be high quality as Subway proves (paragraph here)

BONUS TIPS – BEYOND THE FOOD

BONUS TIP 1:   EXPLORE THE CUSTARD FACTORY

Despite it's foodie-sounding name, the Custard Factory is in fact a shopping location in Digbeth, Birmingham. It used to be the site of Bird's Custard production, but has now transformed into an urban and unique destination. The Custard Factory is home to Digbeth Dining Club, as well as other independent eateries and shops - and only a few minutes walk from the Bullring, it needs to be on your list of places to visit. My favourite clothing shop in the area is Cow Vintage - you'll see it from a mile away with its bright yellow exterior. It sells, as you might have guessed, vintage clothing and accessories. Expect to see reworked branded items (such as Nike and Ralph

Lauren), as well as one-of-a-kind fashion statement pieces. Digbeth also hosts vintage kilo sales around September, which are so fun to go to. For a small admission fee (around £3 or £4), enter a warehouse full of racks of vintage clothing and accessories. Fill your basket up with as much as you want and head to the checkout, where you'll only be charged a fixed price per kilogram of clothing, no matter what you've picked up! (paragraph here)

BONUS TIP 2:   SHOP UNTIL YOU DROP IN THE JEWELLERY QUARTER

The Jewellery Quarter is home to over one hundred jewellery makers and retailers, who sell bespoke jewellery at a often lower price than high-street competitors. Browse through quaint shops to larger stores filled with unique and often one-of-a-kind pieces. There are lots of restaurants and shops to explore in the area as well, so you'll really be spoilt for choice (paragraph here)

BONUS TIP 3: A BIRD'S-EYE VIEW OF BIRMINGHAM

You're probably expecting this to be a recommendation for a ferris wheel or towering skyscraper, but no - some of the best views of the city can be seen from the Library of Birmingham.

A library may not be on your list of places to visit on any trip, but Birmingham Library is in a league of its own. Constructed in 2013, the library's black and yellow futuristic appearance only offers a glimpse into the modern interior. There are ten floors of areas to unwind with a book and extensive book collections, with the lower floors linked together by illuminated escalators. The top floor boasts stunning views of Birmingham, as well as an impressive Shakespeare Memorial Room. Anyone coming to Birmingham should have a wander through the floors of the library, even if it is just for the breathtaking views at the top floor (paragraph here)

BONUS TIP 4:   THE BEST THINGS IN LIFE ARE FREE

There's so much to do in Birmingham that doesn't cost a single penny. For a showcase of the arts and music, visit the Barber Institute of Fine Arts (open to the general public) on the University of Birmingham campus. Whilst you're on campus, have a walk around the Lapworth Museum of Geology, too, which showcases fossils, dinosaurs and interactive exhibitions. There's also the Birmingham Museum and Art Gallery in the city centre, which has the largest public pre-Raphaelite collection of paintings in the world. The range of over forty exhibitions focus on art to archaeology to social history, so there's something for everyone to enjoy.

If exploring nature is more your thing, Birmingham has over six hundred parks to meander through. One of my personal favourites is Cannon Hill Park, with its amazing views and endless trails to walk through. The MAC (Midlands Art Centre) is also in Cannon Hill Park, which hosts music, dance and theatre events. Some charge for admission, whereas others are free - so be sure to have a look at upcoming events to see what's on offer (paragraph here)

BONUS TIP 5: A FINAL WORD OF ADVICE

After living in the city for my entire life, I have only uncovered a miniscule fraction of things to do here. Birmingham is constantly evolving and changing - that's one of the best things about living in a place like this. My final suggestion for enjoying your trip to Birmingham is not to take things too seriously. Immerse yourself in everything and anything; taste that unfamiliar dish, step out of your comfort zone and do things you've never done before. As I've said a few times in this guide, the fun of travelling is the freedom that comes hand in hand with it; it's the unpredictability of exploration that makes any trip so exciting. Often in life, some of the best memories we make are from those unplanned moments or last-minute decisions. And in Birmingham, well, the world's your oyster (paragraph here)

READ OTHER BOOKS BY CZYK PUBLISHING

Greater Than a Tourist- St. Croix US Birgin Islands USA: 50 Travel Tips from a Local by Tracy Birdsall

Greater Than a Tourist- Toulouse France: 50 Travel Tips from a Local by Alix Barnaud

Children's Book: *Charlie the Cavalier Travels the World* by Lisa Rusczyk

Eat Like a Local

Follow *Eat Like a Local on* Amazon.
Join our mailing list for new books
http://bit.ly/EatLikeaLocalbooks

Printed in Great Britain
by Amazon

76334066R00047